D0211332

Published in 2014 by Dog 'n' Bone Books
An imprint of Ryland Peters & Small Ltd
20-21 Jockey's Fields   519 Broadway, 5th Floor
London WCIR 4BW   New York, NY 10012

www.rylandpeters.com

10 9 8 7 6 5 4 3 2 1

A CIP catalog record for this book is available from
the Library of Congress and the British Library.

ISBN: 978 1 909313 45 3

Printed in China

Illustrator: Gemma Correll
Designer: Jerry Goldie
Editor: Pete Jorgensen

For digital editions, visit www.cicobooks.com/apps.php

CONTENTS

Introduction 4

INTRODUCTION

So, human, you've found my diary and, flagrantly
ignoring all the rules of decorum and general
politeness, you've decided to open it and have
a read through. Well, I can't say that I'm
particularly surprised—humans are not exactly
known for their integrity and conscientiousness.

I suppose you're curious about what it is exactly
that we of the feline persuasion get up to while
you're off galavanting around town, doing
whatever it is you do when you leave the house.
To be honest, once you've walked out the door I
rarely notice you're gone, but, hey, as long as
you're providing the kibbles and the ear rubs, what
you do with your time is your own business, alright?

 Maybe you think that reading
this diary will finally provide
you with some answers to
those many burning questions
you have about cat-kind:
why do we hate hairdryers so

much; what do we really do behind the garden shed; what is that weird smell? I don't blame you for being curious—we cats  are fascinating creatures, after all—but you know what curiosity did, right?

By reading the following entries, you, lucky human, will be gaining a rare glimpse into the life of a truly superior species—a riddle, wrapped in a mystery, packaged inside an enigma, and covered in fur, lint, and dingleberries. These are my purr-sonal diaries, chronicling a year in my dizzying social whirlwind of a life—from fabulous parties to sublime spiritual awakenings, amazing meals to epic naps... oh, so many naps.

However, I must warn you that this diary is completely raw and uncensored—you may learn some rather unpalatable home truths. Are you sure you're ready? Then read on, brave, inferior human, read on. But don't say I didn't warn you...

JANUARY

· · · · · · · · · · · · · · · · · ·

New Beginnings and Artistic Purr-suits

WEDNESDAY 1 JANUARY

Hurrah, a new year! Have already made my resolutions—fully intend to stick to them.

NEW YEAR'S RESOLUTIONS

Will take time to learn new hobbies and better myself.

Will cut down on the catnip.

Will make self useful around house.

Will find new and exciting places to vomit.

Will somehow persuade Dog to go away.

Will convince The Woman to purchase Super Dee-Luxe Kitty Tower™.

~~Will sleep less.~~

FRIDAY 3 JANUARY

Helped The Woman in the kitchen. Assisted with washing up and then started compost heap behind refrigerator with dismembered mouse and small piece of what I think is chocolate but could just be mud.

TUESDAY 14 JANUARY

I have been experimenting with various art disciplines. Have possibly found my Life's calling.

Here are a few of my "pieces:"

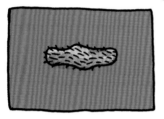

Still Life:
"Hairball on
Pillow, In Red"

Performance Art Piece:
"The Chagrin of Paw Prints
in a Freshly Baked Pie"

Dance:
"Ear Rotations"

Sculpture:
"The Infinite Futility
of Knitting"

Will prob. try litter tray architecture next...

WEDNESDAY 22 JANUARY

Fledgling art career probably over due to unfortunate incident involving The Woman's eye-shadow compact and the (previously) white carpet. Quite upset, as could have been the next Frida Purrhlo or Yayoi Catsuma.

"Self-Portrait While Peeing in
Mrs Smith's Geraniums"
Frida Purrhlo, 2014

FEBRUARY

· · · · · · · · · · · · · · · · ·

Valentine's Day
Furniture Massacre

THURSDAY 6 FEBRUARY

Weird Man keeps coming to my house and distracting The Woman from her important tasks: feeding me, rubbing my ears, and generally catering to my every whim.

I feel v. distrustful of this man.

He calls me "Sweetie" (ugh).

He spends a questionable amount of time fawning over The Dog.

He has villainous eyebrows.

He smells peculiar.

He does not keep treats in his pockets (v. suspicious).

FRIDAY 14 FEBRUARY

Valentine's Day (not that I care)

PET ME

FEED ME

HUG ME

WAKE UP

CUDDLE ME

GO AWAY

MONDAY 17 FEBRUARY

Decided to try hand (well, paw...) at a spot of decorating. Think The Woman will be v. pleased with my improvements.

↑
Upcycled "rustic-style" armchair

Charming lightly distressed pouffe (v. "Shabby Chic")

Tastefully
reconfigured blinds

Lovingly
knocked—over
pot plant

Gently puked—on rug

TUESDAY 18 FEBRUARY

The Woman is not as appreciative of my efforts as anticipated. Have been banished from living room. It's too cold to go outside, so am snuggling in the breadbin, pondering upon post-monotheism and transtheism. (Just kidding! I'm thinking about tuna.)

THURSDAY 20 FEBRUARY

Weird Man came over again. Sat and stared at him, while aggressively licking my genitals.

THURSDAY 27 FEBRUARY

Tried to hypnotize The Dog in an attempt to enslave him and force him to do my bidding. Unfortunately, Dog is apparently too stupid to be susceptible to power of suggestion.

Don't know why I'm surprised, that Dog really is exceptionally imbecilic.

MARCH

● ● ● ● ● ● ● ● ● ● ● ● ● ● ●

Boxes, Selfies, and Laundry Basket Musings

WEDNESDAY 12 MARCH

V. exciting day. The Woman bought new shoes which means new box for me! Hurrah!

FRIDAY 14 MARCH

Used The Woman's laptop to take photos of myself looking adorable in the new box and posted them online. Intend to become a viral internet sensation.

cutiepie 4m

#newbox #nofilter #cute

cutiepie 10m

#Check my new box
#newbox #boxie #YOLO

THURSDAY 20 MARCH

Spent most of today in the laundry basket
pondering some profound philosophical questions.

Confronting these deeply complex thoughts made
me tired, so I took a nap.

TUESDAY 25 MARCH

Frustrating news: internet not yet set afire by box selfies... Maybe I need to get a gimmick.

POSSIBLE GIMMICKS

1. LEARN TO PLAY A MUSICAL INSTRUMENT
Difficult (no opposable thumbs)

2. BECOME CUTE CARTOON CHARACTER
Probably impossible

3. BE GRUMPY
Easy, but it's been done

4. WEAR HATS
Easy, but last resort

5. DO SOMETHING CONTROVERSIAL
Ugh, no way. THIS one is definitely the last resort

Conclusion: ALL too much effort. Nap instead.

APRIL

Bathroom Bonanza

TUESDAY 8 APRIL

Raining. Going to stay indoors and chat online with international friends.

CAT CHAT   @Connect   @Discover   @Meow

TIDDLES
@tiddlez
"Hug Life"

Trends
#Love Catnip
#NoBath
#brb
#EarwaxParty
#salmon
#tuna
#chicken
#hungry
zzzzzzzzzz
#SneakAttack

SIR DINGLEBERRY
@sir_dingleberry_the_first
In a sunny spot #amazing

TIGGER
@sassy_cat
@sir_dingleberry_the_first
Hey what's up?

WIGGLES
@wiggles_mcwiggleson
Just spent 2 hours chasing lazer dot. Best day EVER.

TIDDLEZ
@tiddlez
Rubbed my bum on SO many things this morning!

MR PICKLES
@pug_life
HEY GUYS!!! How r u?

TIDDLES
@tiddlez
@pug_life UGH. Go AWAY Dog.

WEDNESDAY 9 APRIL

Still raining :(

MONDAY 14 APRIL

Have noticed that The Woman is much more forthcoming with the treats when she has been drinking wine.*

* Note to self: encourage more wine drinking.

TUESDAY 15 APRIL

The Woman left in a hurry this morning and forgot to close the bathroom door.* Decided to investigate...

* The bathroom has been out of bounds since that unfortunate bidet incident back in 2013.

I found plenty of little things with
which I could entertain myself...

Like this
thing...

And what
the hell is
this thing?

And this thing...

It turns out that
the sink is actually
pretty comfy when
not full of water.
I had a v. enjoyable
four-hour nap.

I even found time for
a spot of exercise.

MONDAY 21 APRIL

I had that dream again :(

I don't want to talk about it.

SATURDAY 26 APRIL

The Woman went out with Weird Man. She knows weekends are supposed to be OUR time. I vomited lavishly into her new handbag in protest.

SUNDAY 27 APRIL

Blamed mysterious handbag puke on The Dog. Ha! He's so stupid he probs thinks he really did it.

MAY

· ·

Party Season

Today was Sticky LePeu's birthday, so we threw a party for him behind the Old Poopin' Shed.

We played a few
party games...

My favorite was "Bobbing for Shubunkins."
I wanted to play "Pin the Tail on the Dog"
too, but the stupid mutt wouldn't stay still.

◄◄ ❚❚ ►► NOODLE's PURR-Ty Mix 🔊▮▮▮ 🐱	
Rock the Cats-bah	The Cats
Let's Dance (and then Nap)	David Meow-ie
Purr-sonality Crisis	Mew York Dolls
Fishylicious	Destiny's Kitten
Songbird (I'm Going to Eat You)	Flea-twood Mac

SATURDAY 3 MAY

Sticky got some fabulous gifts. I am quite jealous.

A TEENAGE BOY'S SHOE
From Sir Dingleberry

THEATER TICKETS
From Smudge

TROUT!
The Musical

A JAR OF FERMENTED RAT
TAILS IN FISH BRINE
From Sticky's cousin, Juan
(it's a Spanish delicacy,
apparently)

colas
de rata

FANCY BOTTLE OF
VINTAGE TOILET
WATER
From Mr Buttons

finest

THE
Litter
BOX

And, from yours
truly, a subscription to
Europe's premier feline
style and gossip magazine.

SUNDAY 11 MAY

Had to spend several precious napping minutes online de-tagging unflattering photos of me from Sticky's party.

JUNE

Pseudo-moths and Text Messages

Smudge came over to play our favorite game: "Knocking Stuff Off Shelves."

HOW TO WIN POINTS (demonstrated by Smudge)

Head nudge
+ 5 points

Paw push
+ 10 points

Tail flick
+ 15 points

Body shove
+ 20 points

Lands on floor
+ 5 points

Lands upright
+ 10 points

Lands upside
down
+ 15 points

Lands on dog
+ 50 points

Breaks
+ 25 points

I was winning 250 points to 195, but The Woman came home and seemed a bit upset about the broken pot thing, so game had to be abandoned.

WEDNESDAY 4 JUNE

The Woman says Smudge is not allowed to come around here anymore.

I am stealthily farting on her pillow in protest. →

THURSDAY 19 JUNE

Spent most of day chasing moth around living room... Turned out to be a piece of fluff.* Still, an enjoyable few hours.

* In my defence, it was a VERY moth-like piece of fluff.

WEDNESDAY 25 JUNE

The Woman left her phone at home. Took the opportunity to send a few v. important text messages...

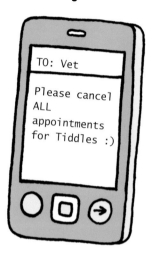

TO: Vet

Please cancel ALL appointments for Tiddles :)

TO: Weird Man

YOU SMELL! Please don't call me again.

TO: All

Dog free to good home. Even mediocre home will suffice.

TO: Boss

JULY

Spiritual Awakenings
(and Naps)

WEDNESDAY 2 JULY

Like all those of the feline persuasion,
I am v. in touch with my spiritual side.
I have been working on balancing my Chatkras
(discovered 3rd Eye was blocked by hairball).

KNOW YOUR CHATKRAS
(Each Chatkra governs certain areas)

Consciousness, enlightenment, and fear of the vet

Visions, telepathy, and ability to hear can opener from half a mile away

Sound, expression, communication, and eating

Creativity and napping

Love, trust, and scratching

Energy, power, and pouncing

Not a Chatkra (just mud)

Survival, security, and bum-licking

Visit from best friend Charlie.
Charlie is a renowned expert in the ancient feline arts of Kitty Feng Shui, Catstrology, and Meowism.

PRINCIPLES OF KITTY FENG SHUI
By Dr Charles Tiddlywinks

The litter box should be placed in a prominent position to stimulate the flow of good ch'i and enable you to stare at the humans while pooping.

The kitchen is the most important room in the house.

A full food bowl is the most favorable.

A well-positioned box encourages positive ch'i.

PRINCIPLES OF KITTY FENG SHUI

By Dr Charles Tiddlywinks

The most auspicious spots in the house should be kept clear and free from energy blocking debris (i.e. all humans and dogs).

IMPORTANT NOTICE

Positive energy flow can be disturbed by loud or annoying noises. Look out for:

Vacuum cleaners

Small children

Hairdryers

Folk music

THURSDAY 10 JULY

In a quest to achieve spiritual enlightenment, I have also been practicing Catha Yoga under the guidance of esteemed Yogi, Snugglemuffin.

CATHA YOGA POSES

The Downward-facing Parp

The Scratching Tree

The Lick 'n' Twist

The Rolling Bend

... and, of course, my personal favorite,
The Sleeping Cat.

AUGUST

· ·

Entre-purr-neurial Skills

FRIDAY 1 AUGUST

Spiritual enlightenment is great and everything, but sometimes a cat needs material THINGS. Things like toys and cans of salmon and those little bits of plastic that come off bottle tops.

Then there's the matter of the Super Dee-Luxe Kitty Tower™, the ownership of which is, I believe, my inalienable right as a feline being.

I spent the entire afternoon rearranging The Woman's magnetic poetry kit* on the refrigerator door in order to make desires v. clear. Sadly it was ignored, as usual.

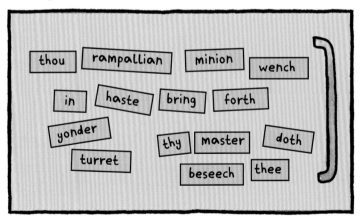

* I did have to make some slight compromises as it was the Shakespeare kit.

Decided to sell a few things on Catslist.
Hopefully I will raise enough funds to purchase
a Super Dee-Luxe Kitty Tower™ as does not
seem to be forthcoming despite hints.

Selling (9)   ∧ ∨

Handmade OOAK necklace   211.99
HAIRBALLS *Shabby Chic)   0 bids
Organic fair trade natural

Collection of pen lids   9.99
RARE *VINTAGE* VGC   0 bids
collectible
Slightly chewed

ANNOYING dog !!!! bargain   0.99
Used L@@K wow 0.99 ONO   0 bids

Express delivery available
Free P&P

V. disappointing response so far...

MONDAY 18 AUGUST

Catslist items did not sell... Some creatures have NO taste. Hmph. Will have to rethink money-making strategy.

IDEAS FOR MAKING TONS OF MONEY

Modeling
(of the "artistic" variety only)

Sell body as advertising space

Write a salacious tell-all blog that leads to book deal

Illegal back-street gambling

Maybe I should just get a job...

HA HA HA HA HA HA HA HA HA HA HA HA HA HA HA HA HA
HA HA HA HA HA HA HA HA HA HA HA HA HA HA HA HA HA
HA HA HA HA HA HA HA HA HA HA HA HA HA HA HA HA HA

Just kidding! Jobs are for inferior creatures like horses, dogs, and humans.

SEPTEMBER

A Fruitful Month

WEDNESDAY 3 SEPTEMBER

Invited the girls over for
cocktails and nibbles.

Made some yummy canapés...
Am a domestic goddess!

Next door's goldfish,
Goldie, atop a bed of
cream cheese.

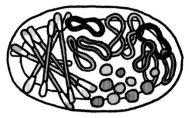

Platter of used Q–tips,
elastic bands, and dog kibble.

Crème d'oreilles de souris
bruschetta

Puréed catnip
compote

THURSDAY 4 SEPTEMBER

Ugh. Really overdid the catnip yesterday.
I feel terrible now.

Today I will consume only kibble and bites of
the houseplants.

WEDNESDAY 10 SEPTEMBER

Was bored, so spent the morning individually
licking each piece of fruit in the fruit bowl and
then putting it back in its original position.

FRIDAY 12 SEPTEMBER

Day mostly spent looking admiringly at myself in the mirror.

I am truly a magnificent specimen of felinity.

OCTOBER

A Most Regrettable Occurrence

Decided to read some books today.

The Woman's collection leaves rather a lot to be desired, I must say.

TO KILL A MOCKING BIRD

★☆☆☆☆

Misleading title

LASSIE

★★☆☆☆

Meh

Eat Sleep Poop

★★★★☆

Inspiring

Mum's DIARY

★☆☆☆☆

Zzz. BORING

Of Mice and Men

★★☆☆☆

Not enough mice

How to rule the WORLD

★★★★★

BRILLIANT!

TUESDAY 7 OCTOBER

Went over to Princess Snugglemuffin's place for a quick drink.

(They do the BEST two-day-old stale apple juice over there.)

Of course, one "quick drink" turned into ten and before I knew it we were gallivanting around the neighborhood, pooping in flowerbeds and singing and chasing our own tails and...

Well, then my memories become a little hazy...

Woke up in Dog's bed with NO IDEA how I got there.

Hmmm.
Where am I?

OH, DEAR GOD....

Managed to creep out before The Woman noticed, thank goodness—I would never hear the end of it.

MONDAY 13 OCTOBER

After last week's regrettable occurrence, Dog seems to be under misguided impression that we are now "friends."

FRIDAY 17 OCTOBER

Ugh...

THURSDAY 30 OCTOBER

Princess and I made our Hallowe'en costumes.

"Human"

CAT TUBE

LOL
OMG
<3

👍 100 👎 0

"The Internet"

FRIDAY 31 OCTOBER

Went trick or treating with the gang. Not a bad haul:

One set of jiggles

Two flying fripperies

One pair of doohickies

One fandangler

Finally, a fine selection of doodads

I will add all of these to my under-the-sofa thingamajig repository.

NOVEMBER

· ·

An Unexpected Vacation

WEDNESDAY 12 NOVEMBER

The mobile torture chamber has appeared in the hallway... This can only mean bad things.

THE MOBILE TORTURE CHAMBER

AKA "The Vessel of Terror"

AKA "The Clink"

AKA "The Devil's Box"

AKA "La Bolsa de la Muerte"

MONDAY 17 NOVEMBER

ABANDONED... The Woman has left me. Endured some terrible, awful things. Events that no cat should ever have to experience. I am traumatized and will prob. never recover.

TUESDAY 18 NOVEMBER

The Woman bought treats.
I am suddenly feeling much better.

DECEMBER

Santa Claws is Coming
to Town

I wrote a letter to Santa Claws...

Dear Santa Claws,

For Christmas, please bring me the following:

1. Super Dee-Luxe Kitty Tower™
2. Cans of salmon (at least 38)
3. Selection of elastic bands
4. Catnip (the fancy sort)

I have been v. good all year. I only ate two and a half pot plants and those were really mercy killings—those plants were ugly.

Yours meowingly,

TIDDLES

 P.S. Please take Dog away.

The gang and I got together to celebrate the season with some customary feline festivities:

Babsi brought traditional Austrian "Vogeltörtchen."

We gathered around the scratching tree to play "Swipe the Bauble."

We enjoyed some delightful yuletide beverages, such as Tinned Tuna Nog, Hot Salmon Cider, and Mulled Out-of-date Salami.

Of course, we all participated in the traditional "Running of the Dog."

TUESDAY 16 DECEMBER

Made a very special Christmas present for The Woman. It's just one of her favorite sweaters, except now it's been embellished with lots more of my fur!

Tried to use The Woman's credit card to purchase gift for Dog, but I couldn't crack the password—it wasn't my name... disgraceful!

ONE—WAY
TIMBUKTU

This is what I wanted to buy Dog. I will have to go with Plan B: a selection of litter tray nuggets.

WEDNESDAY 17 DECEMBER

Entertained and delighted the neighborhood with an impromptu 4am Christmas-carol sing-a-long.

WEDNESDAY 24 DECEMBER

I hope that box under the tree is the Super Dee–Luxe Kitty Tower™.

THURSDAY 25 DECEMBER

It is! It is the Super Dee–Luxe Kitty Tower™!!! ARRRRGGHHHHHHHHHH! SO excited!!!

Life is complete!

FRIDAY 26 DECEMBER

Ummm.... Think I prefer the box, actually.

ACKNOWLEDGMENTS

Thank you to everybody at Dog 'n' Bone, especially to my editor Pete Jorgensen and designer Jerry Goldie.

As always, big thanks to all of my friends and family, to Anthony, and to the pugs.

This book is dedicated to the memory of Ollie, the best cat friend that I ever had.